DATE DUE

OC 4 '04			

DEMCO 38-296

The publisher gratefully acknowledges the generous contribution to this book provided by Charlotte Hyde and Jean Sherman and by the General Endowment Fund of the Associates of the University of California Press.

FOR

NEW CALIFORNIA POETRY

EDITED BY

Robert Hass
Calvin Bedient
Brenda Hillman

For, by Carol Snow
Enola Gay, by Mark Levine
Selected Poems, by Fanny Howe

ıς

FOR

Carol Snow

UNIVERSITY
OF CALIFORNIA
PRESS   Berkeley   Los Angeles   London

Berkeley and Los Angeles, California

University of California Press, Ltd.
London, England

© 2000 by
The Regents of the University of California

Library of Congress Cataloging-in-Publication Data

Snow, Carol, 1949–
    For / Carol Snow.
        p.   cm. — (New California poetry : 1)
    Includes bibliographical references.
    ISBN 0-520-21783-7 (alk. paper). — ISBN 0-520-21784-5 (pbk.:
alk. paper)
    I. Title.   II. Series.
PS3569.N57F67   2000
811'.54 — dc21   99-16317
                                                                CIP

Printed in the United States of America

08 07 06 05 04 03 02 01 00 99
10 9 8 7 6 5 4 3 2 1

Photograph on pages ii – iii by Dale Going. Reproduced by
permission.

The paper used in this publication meets the minimum
requirements of ANSI/NISO Z39.48-1992 (R 1997)
(*Permanence of Paper*).

For the teachers.

Especially MFE, RH, and JK.

CONTENTS

FOR

NEWS OF

News Of

another massacre; and the clean bright morning.
Keeping walking. 'Contradiction' is human—I know that.
And 'knowing' . . . A stirring from the place the whirlwind—something
   like fear—arises, and watching my breath

to still that. Suddenly thinking somewhere in the breath—along
the breath, is an *understood* place. Somewhere—but somewhere
in passing—where the matter is reconciled.

News Of: Codicils

Too many things

one must know — so many —

a place on the breath for each? each passing?
(its turning — breath's inmost
turning, my Love —

for delight —)

*

And another

"massacre of the innocents."

And that there is a form
even for that.

*

Breath as

tidal — ardor . . . fervor . . . horror . . . as moon —

*

What comfort?

*

There was a moment

of blessing, calm.
Though it was a pause, a hiatus.

*

"*. . . then what felt like a whirlwind*

had risen up
in me, such that

little was spared."

*

News of

the unbearable, happening.

Breath saying *Now, now.*

TETHER

Tether

It ran from me, its tether dangling.

No: it ran from me, I had only the loose tether.

Positions of the Body VI

Wanting not only the stillness of hills
but intercession—as by new grass

on the hills—with the silence
towering over the hills, Moore sculpts a massive

figure in black marble: a woman's
body, reclining, curved; eloquent

as bone, shell,
stones worn beyond contradiction.

*

                              You stopped
by the roadside, hills

lying in middle distance, few houses. Only the green
reaches of vineyard intervening

seemed manageable, that is, human—a matter
of scale; the silence was huge, so that only

the hills (which were huge,
also) could rest.

Cézanne, leaning to his canvas, would have mastered
that view, you thought: the blues and greens
and ochres of proximity and distance, that tenuous

position in the dance, not of the drawing
together of unlike, like bodies, but of the holding
apart of the body and terrain; you were held

so still, you thought that you might become those hills,
or must have been borne by hills,

or maybe your body
had been a maquette for the hills.

Mask Series

1.

The hills and I would exchange qualities.
(In my need.)

Which frank, which masked?

If I were over there by the boats?

2. *If I were over there by the boats?*
(displaced . . . 'withdrawn' . . .)

                              Or drawn to memory by a vague memory
of walking to the front of a crowded room to receive
(a laurel leaf stapled to a postcard) my prize
in the contest of naming a series of natural objects
placed in a box, a closed box: by touch alone,

day after day in camp: 'pinecone,' 'chestnut,' 'burr,'

'?': deep in the blindness of the inside of the box (apart, in a kind of
    listening; the glaring, the dusty
world, displaced . . . 'withdrawn' . . .)?

*

Tethered—by touch—to the level
of form (the fingers, stubbed at form, all attention at the edges)

to recognize—by touch—by a likeness
of form (which is not 'to remember'):

where the eyes were looking was *for*.

    Bereshith [In the beginning] . . .

    God wanted to behold
    God . . .

    and turned to fragments . . .

(A card I found at the back of a drawer—the leaf
then dry, yet fragrant.)

3. *Which frank, which masked?*

facing (as facing hills),

engrossed—

The expression of looking at—beautiful, 'available'—

                                                 "Beatrice
gazing upward and I on her . . ."
Beatrice in suso, ed io in lei, guardava . . .

Passing men,
the woman does more than look down or aside;
she looks away and also changes the shape of her mouth.

Dearest.

The thought of you looking away and fear
rose in me—as shame rises—as into lack.

And trees seemed

hollow, then—all glory, all

attention, drained out—drained
suddenly as though violently

poured—

Rabbi Isaac said,
"The light created by the Blessed Holy One in the act of
Creation
flared from one end of the world to the other
and was hidden away."

. . . Rabbi Judah said,
"If it were completely hidden
the world would not exist for even a moment!
Rather it is hidden and sown like a seed
that gives birth to seeds and fruit . . .
Since the first day it has never been fully revealed. . . ."

David—having climbed the stairs
to bed, his breathing a little
'pronounced' (recognizably his breath)—David

pulling the fabric of the nightdress down
over the curve of my thigh (he loves)
and stroking the soft flannel.

4. *The hills and I would exchange qualities. / (In my need.)*

But 'assume,' not 'exchange': "I would assume /
qualities of the hills. //

Solidity. Glory. Repose (in my need)."

                                               But not

'qualities'—rather,

'attributes' . . .

Sequence (Triptych)

Temporary reflectors were embedded in the new
asphalt. Flimsy in the day. Metallic petals
recalling rose petals they followed—I wondered where to put them—
which floated to my skin and stuck almost skin-colored, "sterling" re-
    blooming in hot, wet . . .

somehow I am fourteen and panicking. Disorder in *the making*
and *the order of.* Florid but actual. Pink-looking. Pink against the actual

skin. Driving, reflectors on the left; envisioning the petals they
    succeeded, somewhat larger in a central
panel; my body as I saw it in the water, in the panel
on the right: if one encountered them together. Petals,
loose in a bowl, long-dried, then I threw them in the bath—an
    afterthought—

Asides

I'd wanted to 'stack' three images so they were perceived sequentially, like frames of a cartoon, and also hierarchically;

the stack would be read from top to bottom, like text, and therefore the weight of conclusion would fall on the lowest (last) image;

not a story, though: a *complex*—though one which might be criticized, were it presented as I conceived it (as a visual arrangement), as *literary*.

*

Two photographs printed one above the other on a page: headshots— these were subjects/models for the painter Francis Bacon—heads turned at his behest, since the shoulders are roughly square while the faces turn as far as seems possible stage right (an Egyptian effect). Interestingly, the man's one eye aims down and back as though 'guarding his flank' (that side of his face), while the woman (beneath) gazes yet further in the direction of her head's turning (possibly graciously).

During our conversation the poet's turning her face to one side when she spoke of "the voices": to utter from privacy, from the provenance of *voices*, I expect, and only possibly to observe the world ("a little movement in the streets, in the shops") at that moment through the café window.

Bernini's *St. Teresa* as I have seen the sculpture in color plates: eyes closed, her head thrown back and rolled in an ecstasy of epiphany (beside her the angel raising its arrow to pierce her).

*

The Bacon photographs I saw in a book recalled my friend's turning aside, their placement on the page perhaps suggesting the 'stack' form.

The turning aside (my friend becoming the observed/the model) which lent intensity to her words so they later haunted me.

The sequence not one of *increasing acquiescence*—where the middle section would be anomalous—but of *decreasing volition,* and finally erotic.

Conversation

"Yet with a slight shift of will . . . ,"
confiding she couldn't say no to her mother. Still. Even in the dream.
Then insisting on declining the half of a ripe fig
her friend offered and she wanted.

On His Therapy

He said, "I talk and talk and my talk feels like bullshit."
Then, "But what I picture then describe . . ."

Then Three Reflections

Six pilings. Three pairs which had anchored a small pier
stored—bleached—at the first winter storm.

(Early, this year.)

Imagine recalling.

Shadows?—reflections—of three (the row of them
nearer, seen at an angle from the shore)

approached like moonlight on water (without seeing), approached your
    seeing.

—There was wind, a slight roiling of the water of the fjord—

Imagine (arms and hands) waving frantically.

The glare—where the pilings
entered deeper water and continued, hinged—swathed

by dark shades: toward their tips (the tops of the pilings, projected)
    less certain,

tearing where they reached.

Actually: paralyzed, frantic.

While a piling in the shallows cast a rift or lapse
in the glossing of the surface; so through water in its shape (also

tearing, nearing) you could see the stones of the beach clearly.

The Rod

Her father pulling her arm to take her to punish her and the girl's
resistance made something like a rod stretching from her shoulder
to the wrist he had hold of.

And the life she began there—her attention taken lately with broken
reflection in the harbor—seems freighted and digressive.

And its pulling to that from that makes something like a rod.

Memory

Where the window should be, curtains are.
But the looking is—the movement of looking—
despite a rotation of planets.
I feel most rested when my mother and I lie on my side.

For K.

Then Kathy—"Is that mine?"—ran out to the crying in the yard.

Recollection

In part in a child's voice yet somehow in my voice—my voice as a
     child?—in confidence
to an officer taking her deposition in the mystery,
the actress—playing a 'tart'—recalled sexual hurt but beneath that,
hurt. "I didn't like it": almost a plea, almost
ashamed; I kept hearing the actress's voice—or her part—-saying, "I
     didn't like it," though by then I was seeing:

> . . . When I had exhausted the garden, and a greenhouse
> with nothing in it but a fallen down grape-vine and some

—at the end of a page of *Great Expectations*—which I read aloud so it
     would take precedence.

Helpless, behind Her

A woman on the platform across—my train would continue—facing
away;
the fall of her long black hair continued to seem to me a starting place,
and moving—

helpless, behind her, its flowing a falling upon (so a table or ledge or
caress where the shoulders) . . .

And I'd thought of the gathered style as sweet—which I studied from
the back of the lecture hall (unseen—blameless), the young
women in a new style of hair tie, elastic and fabric—hair gathered up

for falling; my hands know the cradling and gathering—recalling
attention where my mother attended—the warmth of one's palms at the
small
warmth at the back of one's head, it is very

private. How, sweet? As promise . . .

Years of therapy and beginning to notice my habit of switching off the
lights, setting a cup down, putting up the knife
in an area behind me—starting away (not witnessing—blameless), an
arm stretching back—

fumbling, often; having to go back and begin again but already
departing . . .

Pretty fabric clustered, bright hair . . .
Sometimes cradling my husband's head, or Kathy's (small, my not
    knowing a child's head) . . .
Then remembering the young woman I was—yes, suffering; others
    mistaken—

I pictured the back of a head suddenly, dark hair, small as though seen
    from a vantage
(I had relented). . . .

Dear

It's hard, though, to give up
belonging (to). And wasn't our attraction
real? Although we were 'bound'—father and daughter—
although, or because, or it's facile to say so . . .
'stock' . . . apparent. The familiar's
gone now; the eyes must determine, determine, always
looking (for) . . .

(5/9)

As though my shadow were taking a shape—that I should guess at
that shape and become it?—inchoate, animate, a Golem my back's
    always
turned to: his decline, proceeding . . .

(5/10)

I said: *No, no. No.* And made every gesture—the head, a hand off the
wheel—*no*, the whole drive home (alone). The little
vocabulary! (as when I learned him—early), the repetition (as in
    learning
to identify—that, from the first). I said: *No, no . . . not in me;*
and then it is fear, I begin to breathe heavily. I think he is wanting me.

(5/11)

There isn't the time to think about this. Every time I sit still.
The ginger eyes of the ginger stray—face all scratched, the queerly
    outsized head, he came to the back door—somehow
familiar: what was wanted from me? (I feared I would be 'adopted')
    his cry,
importunate; and what I wanted—*I:*—detachment; only an episode,
    how to extricate myself . . .

*

What memories? Affection when I was admiring him.
When I was admired: he could be proud of me. And he brought me
    presents.
So say that he loved me. Or loved my behavior. Certain behaviors.

*

I was feeling a little better and now, not.
A raccoon trashed the lily: the strew of pink petals in the pond.
A broken branch in the Chinese poem in World Lit. in high school
    which meant her virginity was lost, which was lost on me.
Now the mood, the day, the blossom, my illusions; and paper picks up
    the debris as in training a dog.
Or *a skimming of things off the top*—like the petals, like fat (I keep typing
    'fate') or like mold . . .
Why so upset? Things are still 'related.' Ah—

(5/12)

31

We can talk a little, okay? But only a little—a skimming
a surface. Under a bridge but over the reflection of the bridge
in that painting you so admired—one of the pair, Dutch (you owned).
     (So much
in our shared look: wit, elation, intimacy—that you recognized me?; I
     resembled . . .)
How you liked the Impressionists, too—their reflection, refraction,
     more difficult—(not to say 'loved'). (I thought to belong in that look
forever . . .) Though your Boudin turned out to be forged—a poor
     investment—not even a copy,
since the original of that painting never existed . . .

                                                            (5/13)

I was reading, interested. Quiet.
The sun on the back of my head, my neck: a caress. I was acceptable
     here.
The line of my neck as though drawn, I was still, calm, where the light
     fell. Accepted.
The warmth on my neck where the light fell, behind me, the line of my
     neck after his, which he gave me, accepted: a caress.

                                                            (5/14)

Then the next I imagine myself drawing up out of these limbs
I inhabit as though something if not the marrow—the intent—were
     not his . . .

                                                            (5/15)

Pool

Saw (into) and entered the wide corridor.
(Narrow room.)

Attracted by the promise of the purity of 'figure and ground.'

". . . and the blue beside the white in the striping is the color / of the
river Loire when you read about it in old books. . . ."

Yes, but that stripe or sash of white paper, a scroll
which turned corners—banding walls
'papered' with a brownish burlap—was wide, was water.

I have always adored the sea. And now . . .

                                 And painted blue
paper Matisse had *cut to the quick in color,* he called it, into the contours
    of portions
of bodies emerging from the—overlaid the—white; blue, whole
silhouettes arched like dolphins, expressing abandon—hovered,
    overlapping the—almost abandoning
the frieze, in places:

the frieze adorning the walls recreating Matisse's dining room.

Yes, but the doorways—so also a stretch of lintel
above which *Women and Monkeys* had hung—had been narrowed, so the
    area of the room was contracted.

As time is, in the Museum.

And now that I can no longer . . .

Walls recreating the walls of his dining room,
where Matisse worked on *The Swimming Pool* only in the evenings.

And time, in the work, is contracted.

I have always adored the sea, Matisse said. *And now that I can no longer go*
for a swim, I have surrounded myself with it.

As white.

Yes, but noticed in one corner an area of white for which blue forms
served—not as bodies—as borders but open: walls of a corridor or
banks to a channel
of white, the white itself—'broad' would be a pun—pooled,
recognizably
bodily; and then—

where 'then' was our seeing and moving closer to see more closely—

a passage
where fragments of blue (but almost body almost) fragmented the
white so that
neither color was 'figure' or 'ground'—emblem, banner—anymore,
yet.

Fermata ("Extended Care")

On the TV on in the dayroom of the V.A. "Extended Care" ward where my father was living, an episode of "The Brain" or "The Mind" on memory. On a Sunday; I visited Sundays. Like Matisse's working on his *papier découpé, The Swimming Pool,* only in his dining room only in the evenings? Maybe as different as night and day.

I told him there wasn't a way I could think of for him to leave there. "Write it down for me, then," angrily. I showed him the note and put it in his pocket as though he'd refer to it: "Sandy, this is your <u>home</u>."

A musician (he'd been a conductor) had lost his memory—not just memories: memory—after an injury. From his journal, on camera:

> 4:03 p.m.—At last I'm <u>aware</u>, alive!
> 4:10 p.m.—I have just woken up for the first time!!
> 4:18 p.m.—I exist! I <u>am</u>!!

Entry after entry, exclamations, underlines. His wife, whom he loved desperately every time he met her, escorting him (his walking was time after time to start, stumble and catch himself) to some former colleagues' chamber rehearsal. The quartet playing, his sitting by—his alerts, interruptions, now surprising and extended attention in the music—and listening, rapt . . .

Attendants with newspapers, someone yelling [obscenities] in the bathroom, *me and my Dad*—Dad tied with a sheet to his rolling recliner, the nurse had said "for safety's sake"—side by side in a roomful of men, unwell, most facing the screen.

Why? Why? On the drive back I kept saying why as though there'd been an accident: why did I underline 'home'?

. . . a fermata; rapt, then together the bows lifting and silence, and suddenly the ex-musician's head and torso and arms in a series of spasms, convulsing. Discharging the terrible continuity?

Trying to mitigate the 'this,' the 'is'—

Ophelia's Lament

A penny arcade is my father's grave,
who bereaved me and left me with holidays.
Row after row of round, empty slots:
I do not have the pennies to fill them.

Elegy

And now that I can no longer . . .—no longer have to—
visit him . . .

By the Pond

Reading

by the pond, the immediate—
breath—and then the text, and then the pond.

*

Thought, an intermediate

murmuring—which would be sound (which displaces
sound) but accompanies

sight—

*

Watching the goldfish

(why?)—the body passive,
small eye movements (as though in a dream).

*

Quiet breaths

in a still place. "Each next"
taking up a little of the spill.

*

Many

thoughts, gone.

And the varied
sights, intimate
with these thoughts—

POSITION PAPER

Prone

Nor am I actually lying now on the dock—lengthwise as the dock and also riding its ineffable listing rocking according to wind, waves, currents, tide; occasionally dipping a hand (*Brrr*, maybe I'd swim later . . .) into ripples, like the bottom step of the hinged galvanized ladder entering swells on the dips, into ripples (and my imagining hearing, "That's how you get your plaids")—but recalling—wearing the stunned, ravenous look of Patty Duke as Helen Keller at the pump, one wet hand extended, on the verge of recovering Language? ("Wa . . . wa . . .")—. . . recalling intercourse with the actual. "Ecstasy has its subject/object confusions," I began the poem and there was appreciative laughter from the listeners, to my—it soon became mutual—bewilderment as I read on about hanging laundry. My predilections, my weaknesses! They'd assumed I meant something sexual: when I realized that—the shock of cold water—

Measure

Ecstasy has its subject/object confusions: for instance,
your hand reaching for the line is the line

                              approaching (distance—
closing to the grasped clothespin—[a dancer]
partnering); breath (by which we most

belong: a wavering
            boundary [coastline]; a slip left out to dry already dry, sheer
and fluttering; and breath is *measure*—the passage/the pouring [tether]
of, to—) as and then skirting

ecstasy . . .

*

Loneliness—also—sometimes comprises
distance, breath.

Again this morning

the steering wheel seemed
fragile since not the breadth of my husband's body.

Dedication

Now we are rearranging the garden
both outside the windows and in the garden.
David and I.

Now we are David and Carol.

David in a window imagined the pond
we would place there.
Observing the garden without the pond
or lilies or the pear or the hill.

We have made a clearing, you and I.

So let us be *you* and *I*. Committed to address.
Carol in a window to the empty yard
composed a dedication. *For David:*

loving you as I do—
without skill.

After Sappho

Now

you are a husband's rival.
You in whom this comes to reside.

I Was Reading about Abulafia's "Permutation of Letters"

of the Holy Names and ecstatic inspiration, and making an upside-down-cake with nut genoise batter in my mother-in-law's kitchen (being on vacation). Summer—the "bottom" layer was melted butter, brown sugar and a geometric pattern of blackberries, last year's blueberries (frozen), slices of apple and plum, with pecans as the borders. I halved-again the recipe for the cake—to nine eggs, et cetera—the pan, a roasting pan, that large.

Over and over afterward I imagined having realized the interposition of the fruit—that and the oven rack, placed rather high (I'd thought Judy had some reason), not to mention the halving-again—would alter the timing of the baking.

. . . is the bringing back of letters to their first substance, or materialization, by utterance and thought according to the path of the ten spheres . . .
—The timer went off. And a tester came out 'clean,' although with a peculiar resistance. I could find no platter big enough, so inverted the pan on a baking sheet. Lifted. Briefly, the cake held the shape of the pan. Then a rift appeared among the berries and plums in the middle (of now the "topping"), where eggy ooze rose up, as the edges—at each end of the rectangle a single row of pecans intact—began sliding off the edges of the baking sheet, which had no sides.

Afterward over and over I fantasied the golden lightness of sponge-cake, its ground pecans reiterating the taste of pecans across it. And as insistent, an image of the turning-out—the array of glazed fruits, my glorious arrangement.

Curious that only once, only standing there, did I envision my taking the fiasco out to the trees by the bunkhouse to bury, though that was equally invention.

And how not? I had a reputation.

Yet eventually I scooped what I could of the assemblage, the entirety (all the ingredients were there—), the disorder back into the pan and baked it.

. . . commence to combine the first Name, YOD HAY VAV HAY, and observe its infinite connections and combinations, uplifting and whirling like a cycling wheel, this way and that . . .

And baked it.

"Plates or bowls?"

I said, "Either."

"Should we serve ice cream with this?"

"Sure."

"How delicious!" "Do I taste liqueur? This is divine." (That was probably topping mixed in with the batter.)

I said, "You flatter me."

Three Impromptus

Interrupting the usual view out between two great piers, fronted like a
    phone booth—all door—
a portable toilet, vacant, its door open. Against the horizon of sea, an
    open door

leading into . . . *stub:* it tickled me.

*

An unsettling rattling coming through the ceiling
from the neighbors' at frequent but irregular

intervals—now? (not quite) . . . quiet now? (no)—prediction
driving me distracted that evening, and suspicion (was it something
embarrassing? some sexual 'appliance'?) so I was hesitant to ask.

Though you twist the knob, the ensuing actual
stream of water from a water fountain,

surprises; an arc I expect was a clam's spitting
rising here then there on the tidal flat:
it tickled me. (They'd been playing dice upstairs.)

*

In the game I invented
("Letting") at the prow of a dock,
low tide, midsummer, a very low tide—
prone as so often so the posture
of 'staring into space' was to notice a trickle of stream
emerge from underneath, carrying toward the retreated Canal,
particulate matter: among multicolored sand,
minuscule pebbles, fragments of shell, glass?,
feather, whatever—winning
was to watch the array by one place
steadily, without tracking, not hitching
even on a pink or a particularly catchy brightness
swept past: it tickled
me—or vision—with a lilting
singing against impulse like the clicking
of toy castanets, a stick across pickets,
a playing card at the spokes of a bike.

Four

Arm outstretched, her hand spread like a starfish,
maybe she was trying as hard as she could
to reach the spoon in the tub; I thought she was showing me she was
    trying
as hard as she could to reach it so I would help her.

At the Beach

But kept "—then threw back the shell."

Position Paper

At a high tide, standing behind the breakwater, I found I could position
my gaze very near to—by trying to make out the (submerged)
surfaces of what had been rough beach—the "floor"

so that light sparkling, as off flint, off the incoming swells
below and beyond seemed to hover, over me . . .

I would save someone by intervening.

Or *many* (vaguely), one by one. I would spare,
if not rescue; since by 'intervening' I meant to appear (somehow)

between—as 'would spare' placed me near to a perpetrator
before (I imagined) "his" intended . . . (all of it imagined,

badly: stereotyped poverty class setting, strangers,
an angry, impending . . . the intended . . .)—there, between 'intended'
    and,

you know, 'victim,' I would suddenly surface, absorbing the shout,
    blow,
or shot, even, (somehow) unhurt. That time is over.

Heroic, unscathed; that time, "that toy, that dream, that rest,"
it was already almost over when I saw I could as easily . . .

there would be a woman cradling a child, a child known to her—hers,
    and cherished—and between them
a closeness I'd (somehow) steal into, my looking up intercepting a gaze
    I wanted,

badly . . . It was a joke, really.

That yelling again, that glaring was at me? Miss Absenting Herself, Miss
*   Attention Elsewhere,*
The Dwindler—backing away without moving? Didn't get it, sorry.

(Then sadly, had to miss affection?)

At a high tide—but where to place my having been thinking of
    position?—
I was scared, not sorry—not angry?—

At a high tide, as though just embarked (between waves and
    their . . .)—
but where to place my having been thinking of position?—
I was standing behind the breakwater.

Bowl

Something there. Something
white there under the water.

Tugged on its moorings.

I know, only seen as tugged, my having seen — off the end of the dock

at low tide — half-clamshells nestled among eelgrass, bowls of one
  or two
not yet half filled with sand but almost overlooked; moving by them
  were tiny (baby?) crabs
sidling the tide in. Pincering and nibbling.

I couldn't help meddling.
From a scalp on the dock's underside, I pried a small (young?) mussel,
tough as a thumbnail — denting the soft wood of the dock where I
  crushed it —
but light so that, even in that shallow, it drifted, settling.
Eluding my favorite. I'd chosen a favorite to feed, like a child

at the Petting Zoo, fistful of grass thrust toward the handsomest or
  shyest
or driest deer nose (an offering, something between offering and
  forcing:

'tempting' —) and tracking its deflections . . .

A beetle—the ovoid wash of back with wisps of antennae and finely-
    haired legs—

looking quite real beside the blue-rimmed dish pitched toward us
on its single-stroke base, an oval resting in a wider oval: two almost-
    ellipses
with the character of the brushstrokes of the Chinese characters
in a column on the left—good-humored, somehow . . . *intended,* each
    oval a curve which began to be drawn and was

drawn.

Only seen as tugged: per the Law

of Refraction—with diagrams and "thought experiments"
I struggled to understand this—and the roiling of the water (the
    projecting)
surface per the Laws of Wave Motion, Gravity, and Surface Tension,
that "the universe is composed of atoms," that "a liquid seeks its own
    level,"
per the Laws of About Everything and then the relative clam . . . I
    mean, calm

a viewer on the dock presupposes, the image of a shell
wavered, displaced, but "on its moorings"—flown like a kite, thrown
    like a lariat—

only so far.

"Roll the TV a little closer."

"It'll come unplugged."

"Master of Illusion, Prestidigitation, Legerdemain, Sleight of Hand—"
    His hands

in prayer or *namaste;* thumbs parting to show us the begging bowl
(empty); pinkies hinged, his hands were a bivalve
opening and closing then faster and faster like wings for flight
until—he seemed as surprised as we were—a dove flew out of them!

White as our dove of the Sleight of Water.

We were 'glued to the screen' of the box
showing us this, a variety show broadcast—as television was, then—
in black and white; exciting, therefore,
rhodopsin on the tips of the rods (my short-lived interest in the
    workings
of the eye—remember "the rods and cones"?—

because of the word 'rod').

(Was it the green of trees on the water, the black-green
of the water—licorice-black, licorice-green?)

Fingers following the curve of the inside of the bowl
you were rinsing, so water would go everywhere.

—He'd already "sawn a woman in half." (One saws a *woman* in half.)

There were two columns of line drawings on each page of the
   workbook:

apple	truck
robin	spurs
car	orange
saddle	fir
pine	blue jay

Or:

cow	nest
hen	fishbowl
dog	barn
egg	coop
fish	doghouse

So, hen . . . coop: with an oversized pencil and all your body-mind—
   even the tongue—attending,
drawing around each an awkward loop like a bad lasso (the hand was
   young),

then making the tether.

In a postcard I keep of "Mud Beetle and Blue and White Dish:

Leaf from *Album of Insects and Plants*" —where Ch'i Pai-shih's dish is
    two ovals,
nested—the white of the dish is the white

of the "leaf" (the page). (The begging bowl.)

The dashing magician in white tie—

here memory, as it can, conflates two or more men
in tuxedoes—ran the length of the long table to retrieve another dish—

revving, in passing, the supports of a few of the fifteen already twirling
    ones
(by then the first, the one at the head of the table, wobbling terribly . . .
he barely saved it)—and raced to the foot again to eddy up this last.
    With a fanfare,
before briskly lifting each of them down,
palms flourished he looked out at us, proud—astonishing, really—
he kept so many spinning

on their rods.

Something there. Something
white there under the water.

Tugged on its moorings.

I know, only seen as—seeing (white), tugged:
I am That.

Frame (

Not) dwelling there (but

describing [from
outside] the

) frame

Tour

Near a shrine in Japan he'd swept the path
and then placed camellia blossoms there.

Or—we had no way of knowing—he'd swept the path
between fallen camellias.

In Brief

"—necessitated, you know, by his impairments—"

For

To begin, even in the—even with the—
disarray . . .

An assortment of stones; sand, framed—the "Miniature Zen Garden" a gift
  from my brother—

or even
to be—the difficulty . . .

> (then: "The difficulty to think at the end of day"; but what had
>   reminded me, already, of Stevens? of "A Rabbit as King of the
>   Ghosts"? I dreamt of my mother once as a rabbit—funny—
> but it's my father, clearly: "King" and "of Ghosts," becoming 'a
>   shadow of his former self'—)

to be—

> (that's what it was: "To be, in the grass, in the peacefullest time";
>   confusion
> rallies to my defence "at the end of day"—10/23/90)

stones—of the gift of the garden: "to arrange"—any-which-way on the sand,
the little rake set by.

*

My sister and I, on the phone, were discussing pathos.
She mentioned a line I had written—describing myself—and said, "No
   one should have to suffer like that." That; though describing
the girl I was—so absorbed
in panic it was a kind
of mercy, I said—I'd been trying to argue a kind of mercy.

(Denying?)

   "Hoo, hoo, hoo": a mother—nervous, cajoling, mocking a little—
      making her mouth the mouth of a Mask of Tragedy then breaking
      into laughter, the distress
   of the child—crying, coming toward her, *for*—I guess, unbearable.

And isn't he spared something?—my sister knew I meant Dad—I said I
   thought,
since diminished?
But I had to tell her what had happened, with Dad:

When I came to pick him up he asked me the day and the date. And
   then he wrote these down as a note to himself (you know how his
   hands shake).
So when the doctor called us over, Dad took out this note and read it
   aloud to him: *Today is. . . .* Saying, *They usually ask me this.*

—"Oh, no . . ."

   A mask, aspired to: mere, empty—then the inside of the mask
      turned outward toward you, *for*—something
   heartless the heart goes out to; or, it is torn from you, like laughter.

And we had to laugh.

*

A place chosen as . . . chosen to be . . . made . . .
sacred. Stones

chosen and placed . . .

"*. . . 'mountain-peaks in a sea of clouds,' 'islands in the great sea,' the mother
tiger crossing the ocean with her cubs, . . . even the 'Sixteen Rakkans'*"—
that is, monks who strive for enlightenment in solitude—

each arrangement in its halo—a halted
rippling—of raked sand. Even the space is . . . hushed, in the garden,
along the sequence . . .
hushed at the set relations. Calming, yes? chaos pressed
outward, a swept
path bounding the selected, tended . . .

Tormented, Reb Mikhael shut himself away, weeping, fasting, and
praying *fervently*—until overtaken by trembling—"seeking
[answers to] his doubts." Then his soul ascended or descended
to Pardes and the chambers of the palaces;
or some say, "the chambers of his heart."

Or oysters everywhere on the beach.
And the pried white of discarded shells collecting near the decks of the
beach cabins,
she began to disperse to please me. Re-placing them randomly.
Pattern, habit, the gathered-to-brightness—act by act—dimmed in, by,
her hands.
Nellita: clouds breaking over the Olympics, waves from across the
Canal—

arriving in the almost-rhythm of a sleeper's breaths—subsiding
into breaths at the stony edges. Where we walked along, among—as
    though of—the lapping, fractal . . .

Forbidden his room, "when the men of his house peered between
    the gates[!]," the sage lay motionless—for three days,
Reb Mikhael, *the Angel*—"his body flung down like a stone."

*

Framed in his small room—it was the smallest room the Board and
    Care had—my father, myself, and his ex-wife. Each of us
lacking detachment: Dad intent on his (scrapbook or coins or baseball
    cards) showing us; *sleeping bag, napkins, the smell of urine* . . . Bev
    looking over at my refusing to look over
to her wanting to share a look of shared pity;
my fearing the look—sudden, intrusive—I imagine which would have
    been his glare against my seeing
(a look I imagine—I'll tell my sister—as though *I* cast 'the shadow of
    his former self').

Confusion: to follow to rescue? to escape to escape exile? . . .Whose,
    which body still fending off hurt memory? . . . Denying—but as if
    that were mercy
toward—*for* . . . Your heart "flung down like a stone."

Among stones.

NOTES

POSITIONS OF THE BODY VI
Masters Henry Moore (1898–1986) and Paul Cézanne (1839–1906).

MASK SERIES
Quotes in section 3 are from Dante's *Paradiso,* Canto II, translated by John D. Sinclair (New York: Oxford University Press, 1961) and *Zohar — The Book of Enlightenment,* translation by Daniel Chanan Matt (Ramsey: Paulist Press, 1983). The Zohar was written between 1280 and 1285 and is attributed to Moses de Leon.

ASIDES
"a little movement in the streets, in the shops" is from "In the Evening," written about 1917 by C. P. Cavafy, from *C. P. Cavafy: Collected Poems,* translated by Edmund Keeley and Philip Sherrard (Princeton: Princeton University Press, 1975).

POOL
". . . and the blue beside the white in the striping . . ." is from "Not Going to New York: A Letter" by Robert Hass in *Praise* (New York: The Ecco Press, 1979).

"I have always adored the sea . . ." is "from a statement recorded by Mrs. Alfred Barr, in the files of the Museum of Modern Art" found in the Introduction by John Elderfield to *The Cut-Outs of Henri Matisse* (New York: George Braziller, Inc., 1978).

"DRAWING WITH SCISSORS. To cut to the quick in color reminds me of the direct cutting of sculptors." Henri Matisse (1869–1954) in the text of *Jazz,* translation by Sophie Hawkes (New York: George Braziller, Inc., 1985).

The Swimming Pool, a Matisse paper cutout circa 1952, is in the collection of the Museum of Modern Art, New York.

BY THE POND
"Each next" is from Kathleen Fraser.

PRONE
Patty Duke portrayed the young Helen Keller in the 1962 film *The Miracle Worker.*

I WAS READING ABOUT ABULAFIA'S "PERMUTATION OF LETTERS"
R. Abraham ben Samuel Abulafia (1240–c. 1292) was a Spanish mystic and teacher, author of many major Kabbalistic treatises.

". . . is the bringing back of letters . . ." is quoted in *Kabbalah: The Way of the Jewish Mystic* by Perle S. Epstein (Boston: Shambhala Publications, Inc., 1988).

". . . commence to combine the first Name . . ." is from "The Question of Prophecy," English translation by Jack Hirschman in *The Secret Garden: An Anthology in the Kabbalah* (New York: The Seabury Press, Inc., 1967), edited by David Meltzer.

POSITION PAPER
His Toy, His Dream, His Rest—John Berryman, 1968.

BOWL
Ch'i Pai-shih (1863–1957), sometimes called China's Picasso: his "Leaf from *Album of Insects and Plants*" is in the collection of the Metropolitan Museum of Art.

FOR
"A Rabbit as King of the Ghosts," a poem by Wallace Stevens first published in 1937.

The Zen garden at Ryoanji in Kyoto, Japan, created at the end of the fifteenth century, is a "flat dry landscape garden (*karesansui*) with stone arrangement in seven-five-three rhythm (*shichigosan*) on white sand." That and the various interpretations of the stone arrangement are excerpted from *Japanese Gardens* by Irmtraud Schaarschmidt-Richter and Osamu Mori, English translation by Janet Seligman (New York: William Morrow and Company, Inc., 1979).

The story of R. Mikhael the Angel, a middle-thirteenth-century French figure, and related quotes are from *Kabbalah: New Perspectives* by Moshe Idel (New Haven: Yale University Press, 1988).

ACKNOWLEDGMENTS

My gratitude to the editors of the following publications, in which versions of these poems first appeared: *Antaeus:* "Asides," "Positions of the Body"; *Colorado Review:* "By the Pond," "News Of: Codicils"; *Countermeasures:* "Pool"; *Denver Quarterly:* "After Sappho," "For," "Mask Series," "Measure," "Prone," "Recollection," "Tour"; *Fourteen Hills: The SFSU Review:* "I Was Reading about Abulafia's 'Permutation of Letters'"; *Interim:* "Then Three Reflections," "Sequence (Triptych)"; *Pequod:* "Dear"; *Volt:* "Bowl," "Dedication," "Helpless, behind Her," "Position Paper."

The ten-part "Positions of the Body" appeared in *Artist and Model* (New York: Atlantic Monthly Press, 1990); rights have reverted to the author.

"Mask Series" was reprinted in *The Pushcart Prize XIX: Best of the Small Presses, 1994–1995* (Wainscott: Pushcart Press, 1994).

A letterpress chapbook entitled *Breath As: Short Poems* (Mill Valley: Em Press, 1994) included "*Again this morning,*" "At the Beach," "By the Pond," "Conversation," "Elegy," "For K.," "Frame (," "In Brief," "Memory," "News Of: Codicils," "On His Therapy," "Ophelia's Lament," and "Tether." My thanks to Dale Going for that beautiful book. Em Press also published "Bowl" in its limited edition Poetry Pamphlet Series (1998).

A Fellowship from the National Endowment for the Arts enabled me to attend to this manuscript near completion. I also thank The Poetry Center at San Francisco State University for the support of the 1990 Book Award for *Artist and Model.*

This with heartfelt acknowledgment of David Matchett; Laura Mullen, Brenda Hillman, and each of those who read and responded to this collection over its forming; Kathleen Rendon Hirschfeld; my mother, Adrienne, and my siblings; and kind hosts Judy and Bill Matchett.

Designer: Barbara Jellow

Compositor: BookMatters

Text: Cycles

Display: Scala Sans

Printer and binder: Rose Printing Company, Inc.